Grammar and Vocabulary

This book belongs to

_____

First edition 2013

ISBN 978-981-07-1364-5

Welcome to Learning Express!

Helping your child build essential skills is easy!

These teacher-approved activities have been specially developed to make learning both accessible and enjoyable. On each page, you'll find:

Focus Skill
The focus of each activity page is clearly indicated.

Instructions
The read-aloud instructions are easy for your child to understand.

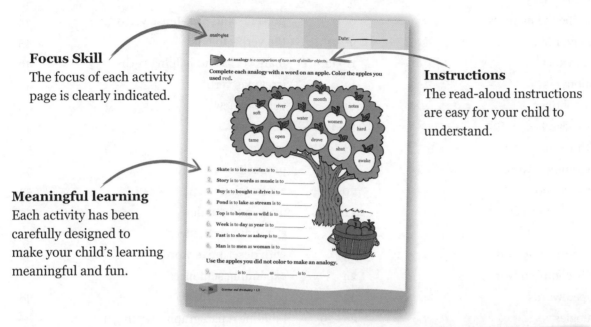

Meaningful learning
Each activity has been carefully designed to make your child's learning meaningful and fun.

This book also contains:

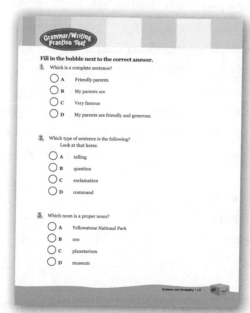

Instant assessment to ensure your child really masters the skills.

Completion certificate to celebrate your child's leap in learning.

Motivational stickers to mark the milestones of your child's learning path.

Contents

Vocabulary

Words! Words! Words! As children learn new words they learn that words can do many things. They can tell directions (above/below). They may tell opposites (up/down). They may name things (elephant/brother). And they can describe things (long, beautiful, silly).

The activities in this section introduce commonly used words that will become part of your child's everyday vocabulary. Children who know lots of words become strong readers.

What to do
Have your child complete the activity pages. Then cut out the vocabulary flash cards on pages 69–73. Review them throughout the year with your child. Have your child add new words he or she learns at home and in school.

Keep On Going!
Have your child find antonyms or synonyms of the words on the flash cards. Also encourage your child to use the word cards to build sentences.

Date: _____

Look at each picture. Circle the word in each row of words that names or describes the picture.

1.

carrot	apple	pencil
black	orange	green
food	far	car

2.

mop	broom	book
drive	sweet	sweep
clear	clean	clap

3.

tree	flowers	flow
leaf	leaves	leap
smile	smack	smart

4.

ducks	doors	cluck
two	three	four
quack	quick	quiet

Date: _____

Look at each picture. Circle the word in each row of words that names or describes the picture.

1.

legs	eggs	ever
sack	crow	cracks
three	six	nine

2.

fish	wish	find
boat	bowl	bow
just	run	jump

3.

candle	cake	can
flame	far	flip
milk	map	melt

4.

bat	boy	bee
dream	drink	drive
woods	wave	walk

Date: _____

Look at each picture. Circle the word in each row of words that names or describes the picture.

1.

horse	goat	zebra
stripes	sticks	stones
after	animal	ant

2.

frog	fruit	from
torn	top	tongue
flip	flap	fly

3.

green	gone	ghost
with	white	while
boo	broom	box

4.

tree	turtle	twist
shed	ship	shell
sit	stop	star

Date: _____

 Antonyms *are words with opposite meanings.*

Read each sentence. Circle the word that means the opposite of the underlined word.

1. You must <u>push</u> the door to close it.
   pull   hit   brake

2. <u>Nothing</u> was in the mailbox today.
   Fun   Everything   Stop

3. My glass was <u>full</u>.
   clear   red   empty

4. I saw a pretty bird <u>outside</u>.
   away   home   inside

5. Susan is always the <u>first</u> person in line.
   second   smartest   last

6. After we <u>work</u>, we will read a book.
   play   study   eat

7. The movie last night made me <u>laugh</u>.
   sick   happy   cry

8. We must be <u>quiet</u> in the library.
   noisy   awake   safe

Date: _____

Read each sentence. Circle the word that means the opposite of the underlined word.

1. We found some <u>large</u> starfish at the beach.
   blue   small   dirty

2. Please do not run <u>inside</u>.
   outside   around   after

3. My friends and I are always <u>together</u>.
   busy   apart   quietly

4. You can <u>stay</u> if you want to.
   talk   rest   leave

5. Do not <u>sit</u> while he is speaking.
   talk   stand   cry

6. My grades are getting <u>better</u>.
   higher   worse   as good as

7. This is a very <u>dark</u> room.
   light   funny   old

8. <u>None</u> of the students went to the play.
   Some   Two   All

Date: _____

 Synonyms *are words that mean nearly the same thing.*

Read each sentence. Circle the word that means almost the same as the underlined word.

1. Tom was outside for <u>just</u> five minutes.

   after   only   over

2. Please <u>save</u> this seat for me.

   bring   buy   keep

3. The three bears lived in the <u>woods</u>.

   forest   house   tent

4. Pam went to bed because she was <u>sleepy</u>.

   quiet   tired   awake

5. I am <u>glad</u> that the flower has bloomed.

   angry   asking   happy

6. First the cat <u>sniffed</u> the food, then she ate it.

   smelled   pulled   pushed

7. Mary <u>tore</u> her best dress.

   mended   ripped   broke

8. The teacher <u>spoke</u> in a soft voice.

   cheered   screamed   talked

Date: _____

All the words in each group are supposed to be synonyms, but one word in each group belongs in one of the other groups. Cross out the word and write it in the correct group.

1. small
   tiny
   joyful

   _____

2. scared
   frightened
   fat

   _____

3. thin
   skinny
   smart

   _____

4. chubby
   plump
   terrified

   _____

5. nice
   little
   lovely

   _____

6. empty
   huge
   big

   _____

7. brave
   daring
   pleasant

   _____

8. slim
   sad
   unhappy

   _____

9. bare
   large
   vacant

   _____

10. hushed
    intelligent
    clever

    _____

11. quiet
    upset
    soft

    _____

12. happy
    glad
    bold

    _____

Words that have more than one meaning are called **homonyms**.

Read the words in the box.

| stem | leaf | root | bark | trunk |

Did you think of a tree? You may be surprised to know that the words are not just the names for parts of a tree.

Write a word from the box that matches both the definitions below.

1. _____

2. _____

3. _____

4. _____

5. _____

(a) the sound that a dog makes

(b) the tough covering of a tree trunk and its branches

(c) plant part that grows from the stem and makes food

(d) turn the pages

(e) stop the flow of something

(f) the part of a plant that holds it up straight

(g) cheer for a team

(h) the part of a plant that grows underground and takes in water and minerals from the soil

(i) the compartment of a car for storing a tire, baggage and other items

(j) the main stem of a tree

Write the missing word to complete each sentence. Then use the definitions from a-j given above that tell the meaning of the word, at the beginning of the sentence.

_____ 6. The _____ was so big that it took 25 steps to walk around the tree.

_____ 7. Our dog will _____ at anyone who stands at the gate.

_____ 8. Which team did you _____ for?

_____ 9. The men used sandbags to _____ the flow of the water.

_____ 10. Why don't you _____ through the book to see if you can identify the tree?

Date: _____

 Homophones *are words that sound the same but are spelled differently and have different meanings.*

Write the correct homophone in each blank to complete the sentences.

1. bored, board

   Some of the _____ students started drawing on the

   white _____.

2. bare, bear

   When a _____ cub is born, it is _____ and its eyes are closed.

3. chilly, chili

   Nothing tastes better than a bowl of _____ on a _____ day.

4. pane, pain

   He cried out in _____ when the glass _____ fell on him.

5. guest, guessed

   Who would have _____ that your _____ was a thief!

6. patients, patience

   I wonder if doctors ever lose their _____ with difficult _____.

7. maize, maze

   Walking through the _____ field was like trying to find our way through

   a _____.

8. hair, hare

   A _____ watched her as she washed her beautiful long _____

   in the stream.

Date: _____

**Circle the space words from the Word Box in the puzzle below.
The words go across and down.**

Word Box

planets	rocket
solar system	astronaut
moon	comet
stars	meteor
sun	galaxy

s	o	l	a	r	s	y	s	t	e	m	p
m	m	e	t	e	o	r	j	c	k	l	l
o	m	o	r	t	i	l	k	o	g	m	a
o	s	q	w	e	r	t	k	m	y	b	n
n	v	s	t	a	r	s	j	e	s	n	e
r	o	c	k	e	t	g	h	t	u	b	t
a	s	t	r	o	n	a	u	t	n	v	s
g	a	l	a	x	y	f	d	s	a	c	x

Date: _____

Circle the occupations from the Word Box in the puzzle below. The words go across and down.

Word Box

CHEF	FIREFIGHTER
TEACHER	BAKER
FARMER	DOCTOR
PILOT	LAWYER
CAPTAIN	DENTIST

F	I	R	E	F	I	G	H	T	E	R	D
A	S	D	R	E	P	W	C	Q	T	F	O
B	A	K	E	R	I	M	A	L	E	A	C
X	C	V	B	N	L	P	P	K	A	R	T
C	H	E	F	O	O	I	T	J	C	M	O
E	R	T	Y	U	T	Z	A	H	H	E	R
D	E	N	T	I	S	T	I	G	E	R	D
L	A	W	Y	E	R	J	N	F	R	A	S

Date: _____

**Circle the math words from the Word Box in the puzzle below.
The words go across and down.**

Word Box

add	borrow
subtract	regroup
plus	sum
minus	difference
equals	math

```
d i f f e r e n c e s q
p w e r e g r o u p u b
l r t y u i o p l k b o
u z a d d f s g h j t r
s x c v n a s u m l r r
w b g e q u a l s u a o
a q m i n u s o h j c w
m a t h i f n d s v t m
```

Date: _____

Use the code to write the missing words.

g	h	v	y	l	n	q	o	e	i	c	t	m	f	u	r	b	s	d	a	w
1	2	3	4	5	6	7	8	9	10	11	12	13	14	15	16	17	18	19	20	21

1. When you ____ ____ ____ numbers, the answer is the ____ ____ ____ .
             20   19   19   18   15   13

2. When you ____ ____ ____ ____ ____ ____ ____ ____ numbers, the
     18   15   17   12   16   20   11   12

answer is the ____ ____ ____ ____ ____ ____ ____ ____ ____ ____ .
     19   10   14   14   9   16   9   6   11   9

3. The words ____ ____ ____ ____ ____ ____ ____ ____ ____ ____
     20   5   12   8   1   9   12   2   9   16

and ____ ____ ____ ____ ____ in a word problem tell you to add.
  12   8   12   20   5

4. The words ____ ____ ____ ____   ____ ____ ____ ____ and
     2   20   3   9   5   9   14   12

____ ____ ____   ____ ____ ____ ____   ____ ____ ____ ____
 2   8   21   13   20   6   4   13   8   16   9

in a word problem tell you to subtract.

5. Two numbers of the same value are ____ ____ ____ ____ ____ .
                              9   7   15   20   5

6. When you ____ ____ ____ ____ ____ a problem, you get the answer.
     18   8   5   3   9

Date: _____

Use the code to complete the sentences below. Then write the number of each place in the correct circle on the map.

e	o	f	a	n	s	u	r	l	m	d	h	c	t	p	i	g
1	2	3	4	5	6	7	8	9	10	11	12	13	14	15	16	17

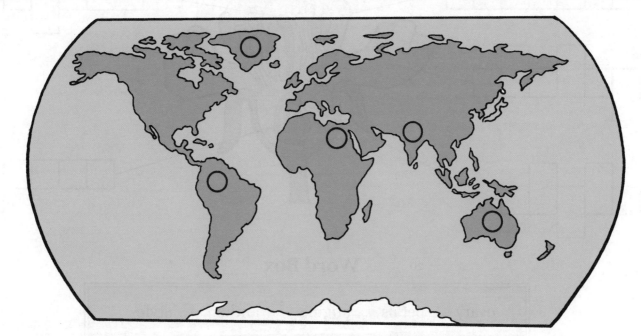

1. The smallest continent on Earth is ___ ___ ___ ___ ___ ___ ___ ___ ___.
    4   7   6   14   8   4   9   16   4

2. The highest mountain on Earth is Mt Everest in ___ ___ ___ ___.
    4   6   16   4

3. The largest island on Earth is ___ ___ ___ ___ ___ ___ ___ ___ ___.
    17   8   1   1   5   9   4   5   11

4. The longest river on Earth is the Nile on the continent of

    ___ ___ ___ ___ ___ ___.
    4   3   8   16   13   4

5. The highest waterfall on Earth is in

    ___ ___ ___ ___ ___   ___ ___ ___ ___ ___ ___.
    6   2   7   14   12   4   10   1   8   16   13   4

6. The coldest place on Earth is ___ ___ ___ ___ ___ ___ ___ ___ ___ ___.
    4   5   14   4   8   13   14   16   13   4

Use the words in the box to label each part of the flower and to complete the sentences below.

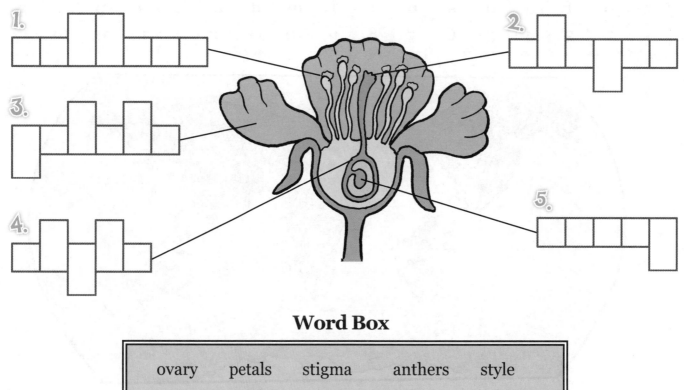

Word Box

| ovary | petals | stigma | anthers | style |

A flower is important in the life cycle of a plant because it contains the parts for

reproduction. The colorful __ __ t __ __ __ and sepals protect the flower when

6.

it is in bud. The sticky part in the middle of the flower is the __ __ __ g __ __.

7.

Around the stigma are __ n __ __ __ __ __ which are tiny stems with knobs on

8.

top. Inside the anthers is a golden dust called pollen. In the base of the flower is the

__ v __ __ __. Growing out of the ovary is the __ __ y __ __. When ripe, the

9. **10.**

anthers burst open sending out clouds of pollen. The pollen is carried to the stigma of

another flower. This is called pollination.

Use the words in the box to label each part of an insect and to complete the sentences below.

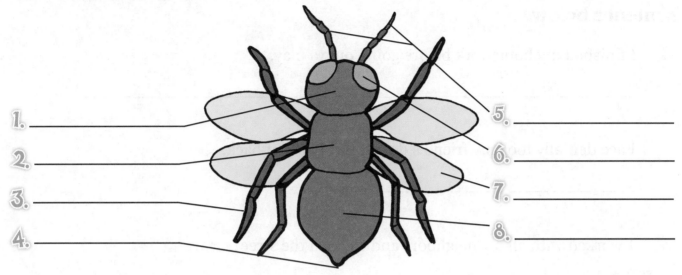

1. _____

2. _____

3. _____

4. _____

5. _____

6. _____

7. _____

8. _____

Word Box

stinger
wings
head
antennae
thorax
eyes
legs
abdomen

An insect's _h_ __ __ __ includes the __ __ _e_ __ and
        9.   **10.**

__ __ _t_ __ __ _n_ __ __. Three pairs of __ __ _g_ __ are
        11.   **12.**

connected to the __ __ __ __ __ _x_ . Most insects
                13.

have one or two pair of __ __ _n_ __ __. The tip of the
                    14.

__ __ _d_ __ __ __ _n_ may have a tube for laying eggs
        15.

or a _s_ __ __ __ _g_ __ __ .
        16.

Write the character trait described in each sentence. Use the words on the caps as clues. Then use the number code to complete the sentence below.

1. I finished my homework before going out to play.

   __ __ __ __ __ __ __ __ __ __ __ __ __ __
     4   7

2. I accidentally took my friend's dollar, but I gave it back.

   __ __ __ __ __ __ __
     2

3. I worked with all my neighbors and cleaned the street.

   __ __ __ __ __ __ __ __ __ __ __
                9   3

4. I asked the new boy to play with me at recess.

   __ __ __ __ __ __ __ __ __ __ __ __ __
     6   5

5. At lunchtime I was very hungry, but I waited my turn in line.

   __ __ __ __ __ __ __ __
            8   1

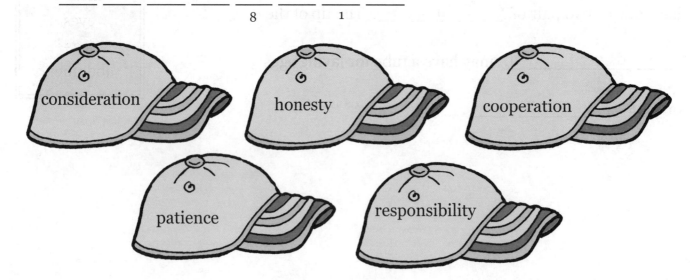

Your __ __ __ __ __ __ __ __ __ is who you are when no one is looking.
    1   2   3   4   5   6   7   8   9

There are many terms related to music that are important to know.

percussion	woodwind	musician
rhythm	conductor	keyboard
composer	string	melody
harmony	opera	orchestra

Write the correct word for each clue. Then write the letter from the boxes in order on the line below to answer the musical question.

1. a person who sings or plays a musical instrument ___ ___ ☐ ___ ___ ___ ___ ___

2. the main tune of a musical piece ___ ___ ___ ___ ___ ☐

3. a person who writes music ___ ___ ☐ ___ ___ ___ ___

4. a play that is sung to music ___ ☐ ___ ___

5. a large group of performers who play classical music ___ ___ ___ ☐ ___ ___ ___ ___

6. an instrument such as a flute, oboe or bassoon ___ ___ ☐ ___ ___ ___ ___

7. a person who directs a musical group ___ ___ ☐ ___ ___ ___ ___ ___

8. pattern of beats in music ___ ___ ☐ ___ ___ ___

What do you call a musical work written for an orchestra? _____

Some words are confusing because they are similar in some way.

Read each sentence and question. Decide which underlined word correctly answers the question. Then write the word.

1. A package just arrived for Jason.
   Did he <u>accept</u> it or did he <u>except</u> it? _____

2. Sam had a sundae after dinner.
   Did he have <u>desert</u> or <u>dessert</u>? _____

3. Beth made a right triangle.
   Does it have three <u>angels</u> or <u>angles</u>? _____

4. All the actors sang and danced the last number.
   Did they perform the <u>finale</u> or the <u>finally</u>? _____

5. Megan swam the length of the pool underwater.
   Did she hold her <u>breathe</u> or her <u>breath</u>? _____

6. Aaron's socks slid down to his ankles.
   Were they <u>loose</u> or <u>lose</u>? _____

7. Jerome just made a dental appointment.
   Should he mark it on the <u>colander</u> or the <u>calendar</u>? _____

8. Lisa opened the gate and watched as the cows ate grass.
   Are the cows out to <u>pastor</u> or <u>pasture</u>? _____

9. Meg addressed an envelope.
   Should she add a <u>coma</u> or <u>comma</u> between the town and state? _____

10. Anna sketched a scene from a story she just read.
    Did she draw a <u>pitcher</u> or a <u>picture</u>? _____

 Are there any words that confuse you? Record them in a notebook. Include the definition and a sentence using the word. Think of ways to help yourself remember confusing words.

Date: _____

Many words have been shortened or clipped over time. Write the shortened form of each word. Then circle the shortened form in the puzzle below. The words go ←, →, ↑, ↓, ↖, ↘ and ↗.

1. laboratory = _____
2. stereophonic = _____
3. champion = _____
4. moving picture = _____
5. referee = _____
6. refrigerator = _____
7. bicycle = _____
8. advertisement = _____
9. veterinarian = _____
10. submarine = _____
11. gasoline = _____
12. automobile = _____
13. examination = _____
14. photograph = _____
15. airplane = _____
16. facsimile = _____
17. telephone = _____
18. teenager = _____
19. mathematics = _____
20. taxicab = _____

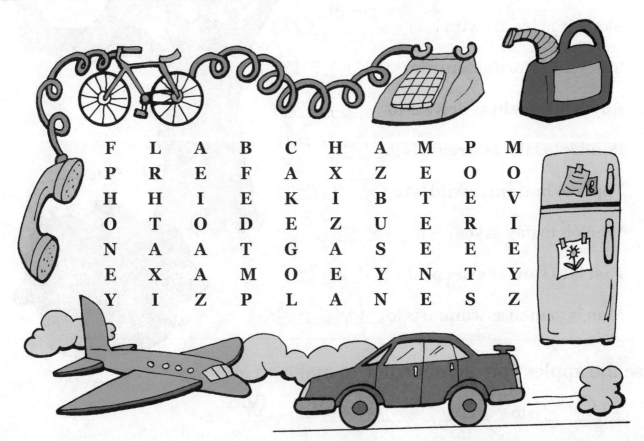

```
F   L   A   B   C   H   A   M   P   M
P   R   E   F   A   X   Z   E   O   O
H   H   I   E   K   I   B   T   E   V
O   T   O   D   E   Z   U   E   R   I
N   A   A   T   G   A   S   E   E   E
E   X   A   M   O   E   Y   N   T   Y
Y   I   Z   P   L   A   N   E   S   Z
```

Date: _____

An **analogy** *is a comparison of two sets of similar objects.*

Complete each analogy with a word on an apple. Color the apples you used red.

1. **Skate** is to **ice** as **swim** is to _water_

2. **Story** is to **words** as **music** is to _note_.

3. **Buy** is to **bought** as **drive** is to _drove_

4. **Pond** is to **lake** as **stream** is to _river_.

5. **Top** is to **bottom** as **wild** is to _tame_.

6. **Week** is to **day** as **year** is to _month_.

7. **Fast** is to **slow** as **asleep** is to _awake_.

8. **Man** is to **men** as **woman** is to _women_

Use the apples you did not color to make an analogy.

9. _open_ is to _shut_ as _hard_ is to _soft_.

Date: _____

Complete the analogy on each bat. Use the words on the caps to help you.

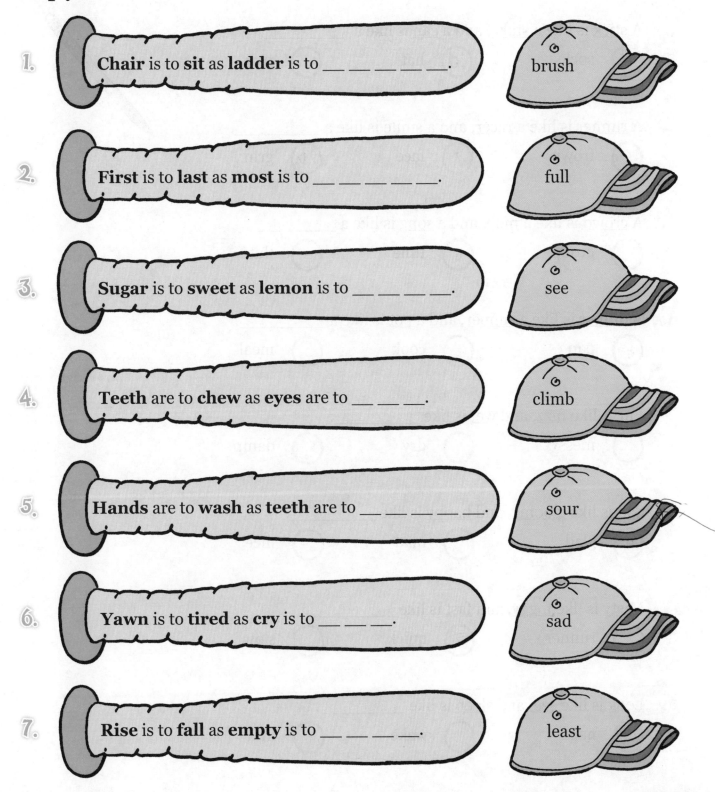

1. **Chair** is to **sit** as **ladder** is to ___ ___ ___ ___ ___.

brush

2. **First** is to **last** as **most** is to ___ ___ ___ ___ ___.

full

3. **Sugar** is to **sweet** as **lemon** is to ___ ___ ___ ___.

see

4. **Teeth** are to **chew** as **eyes** are to ___ ___ ___.

climb

5. **Hands** are to **wash** as **teeth** are to ___ ___ ___ ___ ___.

sour

6. **Yawn** is to **tired** as **cry** is to ___ ___ ___.

sad

7. **Rise** is to **fall** as **empty** is to ___ ___ ___ ___.

least

Date: _____

Fill in the bubble next to the correct word to complete each sentence.

1. A <u>stick</u> is like a <u>stake</u>, and a <u>cap</u> is like a _____.

   ○ sock　　　● hat　　　○ twig

2. A <u>runner</u> is like a <u>racer</u>, and a <u>smile</u> is like a _____.

   ○ frown　　　● face　　　● grin

3. A <u>crowd</u> is like a <u>mob</u>, and a <u>song</u> is like a _____.

   ○ group　　　● tune　　　○ flute

4. A <u>dinner</u> is like a <u>supper</u>, and a <u>pot</u> is like a _____.

   ● pan　　　○ cook　　　○ meal

5. <u>Fur</u> is like <u>fuzz</u>, and <u>wet</u> is like _____.

   ○ messy　　　○ dry　　　● damp

6. <u>Sad</u> is like <u>gloomy</u>, and <u>happy</u> is like _____.

   ● glad　　　○ mad　　　○ nice

7. <u>Misty</u> is like <u>foggy</u>, and <u>fast</u> is like _____.

   ○ runner　　　● quick　　　○ slow

8. <u>Look</u> is like <u>see</u>, and <u>sleep</u> is like _____.

   ● nap　　　○ wake　　　○ find

Date: _____

Fill in the bubble next to the correct word to complete each sentence.

1. <u>Rich</u> is the opposite of <u>poor</u>, and <u>weak</u> is the opposite of _____.
   ○ strong   ○ day   ● frail

2. <u>Give</u> is the opposite of <u>take</u>, and <u>ask</u> is the opposite of _____.
   ○ get   ● answer   ○ teacher

3. <u>Help</u> is the opposite of <u>harm</u>, and <u>work</u> is the opposite of _____.
   ○ hurt   ○ try   ● play

4. <u>Good</u> is the opposite of <u>bad</u>, and <u>rough</u> is the opposite of _____.
   ● smooth   ○ bumpy   ○ mean

5. <u>Over</u> is the opposite of <u>under</u>, and <u>near</u> is the opposite of _____.
   ○ middle   ● far   ○ here

6. <u>Warm</u> is the opposite of <u>cool</u>, and <u>safe</u> is the opposite of _____.
   ○ afraid   ○ cold   ● unsafe

7. <u>Cloudy</u> is the opposite of <u>sunny</u>, and <u>early</u> is the opposite of _____.
   ● late   ○ day   ○ timely

8. <u>Top</u> is the opposite of <u>bottom</u>, and <u>front</u> is the opposite of _____.
   ○ whole   ● back   ○ side

Fill in the bubble next to the correct answer.

1. Chose a word that you might use to describe an apple.

   ○ **A** smart

   ○ **B** juicy

   ○ **C** blue

   ○ **D** tall

2. Choose a word you might use to describe your best friend.

   ○ **A** nice

   ○ **B** striped

   ○ **C** green

   ○ **D** mean

3. Choose the word that is the opposite of **dirty**.

   ○ **A** unclean

   ○ **B** untidy

   ○ **C** clean

   ○ **D** rough

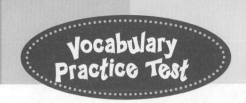

Vocabulary Practice Test

Fill in the bubble next to the correct answer.

4. Choose the word that means almost the same as **ripped**.

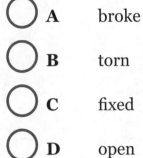

   ○ **A**   broke

   ○ **B**   torn

   ○ **C**   fixed

   ○ **D**   open

5. A fare is the money you pay to ride on a bus.
Which word that sounds like **fare** means to play according to the rules?

   ○ **A**   feat

   ○ **B**   fear

   ○ **C**   fair

   ○ **D**   fore

6. **Socks** are to **feet** as **gloves** are to _____.
Which word completes this analogy?

   ○ **A**   fingers

   ○ **B**   hands

   ○ **C**   arms

   ○ **D**   legs

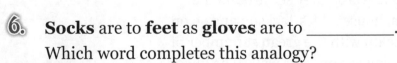

Grammar/Writing

To be successful at playing any game, you have to understand the rules. The same thing is true of writing. Grammar provides the rules your child needs to become a successful writer.

The activities in this section set out the rules for writing. They start with the four types of sentences and the punctuation for each. Familiarity with these is crucial to good writing. Your child will also learn the parts of speech: nouns, pronouns, adjectives and verbs, and how to use them to build clear, interesting and well-developed sentences.

What to do

Each new skill starts with a definition or explanation. Have your child read the definitions or explanations on the activity page. Then have your child complete the activity. Review his or her work together. Let your child know that he or she is doing a great job!

Keep On Going!

Make learning grammar fun! Take a walk together. On your walk, play a game with your child. See who can name the greatest number of naming words they see around the neighborhood: trees, flowers, houses, Mrs Jackson and so on. Challenge each other to come up with the greatest number of words to describe the things you see on your walk: The huge, green, pine tree, full of pointy, brown pine-cones is next to the delicate, bright pink azalea bush.

*A sentence usually has a **subject** and a **predicate**. The **subject** is what or whom the sentence is about. The **predicate** tells something about the subject. The **simple subject** is the main word in the subject.*

A. Read each sentence. Circle the subject and underline the predicate. Then write the simple subject. The first one has been done for you.

Simple Subject

1. (My class) took a trip to the museum. _____class_____

2. Many large paintings hung on the walls. _____

3. Maria saw a painting of an elephant. _____

4. All the children looked at the painting. _____

5. Paul pointed to a cat on a leash. _____

6. His friend liked the dancing zebra. _____

7. The girls laughed at the purple cow. _____

8. Many people visited the museum that day. _____

9. The bus took us back to school. _____

B. Finish the sentences. Add a subject to sentence 1. Add a predicate to sentence 2.

1. _____ was funny.

2. My class _____.

Date: _____

 *A **sentence** is a group of words that expresses a complete thought. A **fragment** is an incomplete thought.*

Write S for sentence or F for fragment.

_____ 1. Insects eat many different things.

_____ 2. Some of these things.

_____ 3. The praying mantis eats other insects.

_____ 4. Water bugs eat tadpoles and small frogs.

_____ 5. Flower nectar makes good.

_____ 6. Build nests to store their food.

_____ 7. The cockroach will eat almost anything.

_____ 8. Termites.

_____ 9. A butterfly caterpillar.

_____ 10. Bite animals and people.

_____ 11. Some insects will even eat paper.

_____ 12. Insects have different mouth parts to help them eat.

A **compound subject** *is two or more nouns connected by* **and**. *A* **compound predicate** *is two or more verbs connected by* **and**.

A. **Underline the compound subject or the compound predicate in each sentence. Write CS above each compound subject and CP above each compound predicate.**

1. Mike and Jody moved away.

2. They often call and e-mail us.

3. Mike jogs and swims every day.

4. Phil and Jan will visit them.

5. Juan and Yoshi moved here from other countries.

6. They speak and read English very well.

7. Lori, Sam and Beth wrote a play about moving.

8. They practiced and presented it to the class.

9. We clapped and smiled at the end.

10. The parents and the principal liked the play.

B. **Complete one sentence with the compound subject. Complete the other sentence with the compound predicate.**

My dad and sister   barked and jumped

1. Buster _____ when we got home.

2. _____ played word games for an hour.

*Every sentence begins with a **capital letter**. A **telling sentence** or statement ends with a **period** (.). An **asking sentence** or question ends with a **question mark** (?).*

Write S for statement or Q for question. Then rewrite each sentence correctly.

1. the sun is the closest star to Earth _____

    _____

2. the sun is not the brightest star _____

    _____

3. what is the temperature of the sun _____

    _____

4. the sun is a ball of hot gas _____

    _____

5. how large is the sun _____

    _____

6. will the sun ever burn out _____

    _____

Date: _____

 A **singular noun** names one person, place or thing. A **plural noun** names more than one person, place or thing. Add -**s** to form the plural of most nouns.

A. **Each sentence has an underlined noun. On the line, write S if it is a singular noun. Write P if it is a plural noun.**

1. She has a new <u>baby</u>. _____

2. <u>She</u> is very cute. _____

3. She has small <u>fingers</u>. _____

4. She drinks from a <u>bottle</u>. _____

5. I can tell my <u>friends</u> all about it. _____

B. **Read each sentence. Underline the singular noun. Circle the plural noun.**

1. The baby has two sisters.

2. The nightgown has pockets.

3. Her hand has tiny fingers.

4. My parents have a baby.

5. The family has three girls.

C. **Complete the chart. Write the singular or plural of each noun.**

Singular	Plural
fence	
	trains
gate	
	cows

*A **common noun** names any person, place or thing. A **proper noun** names a particular person, place or thing. A proper noun begins with a capital letter.*

A.   Read each word in the box. Write it where it belongs on the chart.

Word Box

doctor
park
football
Tangram
Pat
France

	Category	Common Nouns	Proper Nouns
1.	Person	_____	_____
2.	Place	_____	_____
3.	Thing	_____	_____

B.   Complete each sentence with a common noun or proper noun. In the box, write C if you wrote a common noun. Write P if you wrote a proper noun.

1. I threw the ball to _____. (person)

2. I have visited _____. (place)

3. My favorite food is _____. (thing)

4. My family lives in _____. (place)

5. My favorite author is _____. (person)

6. I wish I had a _____. (thing)

7. I like to read about _____. (historical event)

8. My favorite holiday is _____. (holiday)

Date: _____

 A **possessive noun** shows ownership. Add **'s** to make a singular noun show ownership. Add an apostrophe (') after the **s** of a plural noun to show ownership.

A. Underline the possessive noun in each sentence. Write S on the line if the possessive noun is singular. Write P if the possessive noun is plural.

1. Anna's family took a walk in the woods. _____

2. They saw two birds' nests high up in a tree. _____

3. A yellow butterfly landed on Brad's backpack. _____

4. Anna liked the pattern of the butterfly's wings. _____

5. A turtle's shell has many spots. _____

6. Anna took pictures of two chipmunks' homes. _____

B. Complete each sentence with the singular possessive form of the noun in the bracket.

1. Jim wanted to play basketball at _____ house. (Carol)

2. One of _____ new sneakers was missing. (Jim)

3. He looked under his _____ desk. (sister)

4. He crawled under his _____ bed to look. (brother)

5. It was outside in his _____ flower garden. (dad)

6. The _____ lace had been chewed. (sneaker)

7. Jim saw his _____ footprints in the dirt. (dog)

> A **singular pronoun** *takes the place of a noun that names one person, place or thing. A* **plural pronoun** *takes the place of a noun that names more than one person, place or thing.*

A. Underline the pronoun in each sentence. On the line, write S if it is singular or P if it is plural.

1. He is called Spider.   _____

2. I can see Spider has eight long legs.   _____

3. They asked Spider a question.   _____

4. We want to know what's in the pot.   _____

5. It contains all the wisdom in the world.   _____

B. Read each pair of sentences. Circle the pronoun in the second sentence. Then underline the word or words in the first sentence that it replaces. Write the pronoun under Singular or Plural.

	Singular	Plural
1. This story is funny. It is about wisdom.	_____	_____
2. The author retold the story. She is a good writer.	_____	_____
3. My friends and I read the story aloud. We enjoyed the ending.	_____	_____
4. Two boys acted out a scene. They each took a different role.	_____	_____

C. For each noun write a subject pronoun that could take its place.

1. Spider   _____

2. the pot   _____

3. Tortoise and Hare   _____

4. Spider's mother   _____

Date: _____

 *A **pronoun** takes the place of a noun or nouns in a sentence. The words **me**, **you**, **him**, **her**, **it**, **us** and **them** are object pronouns.*

A. Underline the object pronoun in each sentence.

1. Aunt Cindy gave us a football.

2. Our dog Rex found it.

3. He thinks the ball is for him.

4. I said, "Rex, that's not for you!"

5. Aunt Cindy gave me another ball for Rex.

6. Now Rex always wants to play with her.

7. I like to watch them.

B. Decide which object pronoun can replace the underlined word or words. Write the object pronoun on the line.

1. I went to the movies with <u>Rachel and Kevin</u>. _____

2. Kevin asked <u>Rachel</u> for some popcorn. _____

3. Rachel was happy to share <u>the popcorn</u>. _____

4. I accidentally bumped <u>Kevin</u>. _____

5. The popcorn spilled all over <u>Rachel, Kevin and me</u>. _____

6. I said, "Kevin, I'm sorry I bumped <u>Kevin</u>." _____

7. Then I went to get more popcorn for <u>Rachel, Kevin and me</u>. _____

Date: _____

 A **possessive pronoun** *shows ownership or belonging. It takes the place of a noun that shows ownership.* **My, your, his, her, its, our** *and* **their** *are possessive pronouns.*

A. Circle the subject pronoun in each sentence. Then underline the possessive pronoun. Use these answers to fill in the chart. The first one has been done for you.

1. (I) am planning a trip with <u>my</u> family.

2. Will you wear your sunglasses?

3. He will bring his camera.

4. She will take her dog along.

5. It will eat all its food.

6. We will enjoy our vacation.

7. They will show their pictures.

Subject Pronouns	Possessive Pronouns
I	my

B. Underline the possessive pronoun in each sentence.

1. The desert is their home.

2. Her umbrella blocks out the sun.

3. That javelina likes to play his guitar.

4. His address is 1 Tumbleweed Avenue.

5. Coyote said, "My stomach is growling."

6. "I'll blow your house down," Coyote shouted.

7. Its walls are made of tumbleweeds.

8. "Our house is strong," the third Javelina said.

Action verbs *are words that tell what the subject of the sentence does.*

A. Underline the action verb in each sentence.

1. The villagers cheered loudly.

2. They added flavor to the cheese.

3. Please give them the milk.

4. He serves the cheese.

5. He emptied the buckets.

B. Circle the action verb in the brackets ( ) that paints a more vivid picture of what the subject is doing.

1. The villagers (walked, paraded) in the streets.

2. Father (whispered, talked) to the baby.

3. The puppy (ate, gobbled) down his food.

4. The girl (skipped, went) to her chair.

5. The ball (fell, bounced) down the stairs.

C. Write an action verb from the box to complete each sentence.

> whispered   laughed   sighed

1. We _____ at the playful kittens.

2. She _____ deeply and fell asleep.

3. Megan _____ to her friend in the library.

Date: _____

 Present-tense verbs *must agree in number with the subject. The letters* **-s** *or* **-es** *are usually added to a present-tense verb when the subject of the sentence is a singular noun or* **he, she** *or* **it.**

A. **Read each sentence. On the line, write the correct form of the present-tense verb in the brackets ( ).**

1. The crow _____ the pitcher with pebbles. (fill, fills)

2. The man _____ the crow. (watch, watches)

3. Then he _____ the cabbage across the river. (take, takes)

4. The man and the goat _____ the wolf behind. (leave, leaves)

5. They _____ back on the last trip. (go, goes)

B. **Write the correct past-tense form of the verb in the brackets ( ).**

1. J.J. _____ for the hidden picture. (look)

2. He _____ at it for a long time. (stare)

3. Ana _____ by. (walk)

4. Then she _____ him solve the puzzle. (help)

C. **Write three sentences. Use the verb in the brackets ( ) in your sentence.**

1. (play) _____

_____

2. (plays) _____

_____

3. (played) _____

_____

*The verb **to be** tells what the subject of a sentence is or was. **Am, is** and **are** tell about someone or something in the present. **Was** and **were** tell about someone or something in the past.*

A. Read each sentence. Circle the word that is a form of the verb to be.

1. Captain Fossy was Mr Anning's good friend.

2. Mary Anning said, "The dragon is gigantic!"

3. "Its eyes are as big as saucers!" she told her mother.

4. "I am inside the cave!" she shouted to her brother.

5. The scientists were amazed by the remarkable fossil.

B. Read each sentence. If the underlined verb is in the past tense, write past on the line. If it is in the present tense, write present.

1. Mary Anning <u>was</u> a real person. _____

2. I <u>am</u> interested in fossils, too. _____

3. There <u>are</u> many dinosaurs in the museum. _____

4. The exhibits <u>were</u> closed yesterday. _____

5. This <u>is</u> a map of the first floor. _____

C. Write the form of be that completes each sentence.

am   is   are

1. I _____ on the bus with my mother and father.

2. Buses _____ fun to ride.

3. The bus driver _____ a friendly woman.

Date: _____

 *A **main verb** is the most important verb in a sentence. It shows the action. A **helping verb** works with the main verb. Forms of **be** and **have** are helping verbs.*

A. Read each sentence. Circle the helping verb. Draw a line under the main verb.

1. Jamal had built his first model rocket last year.

2. He has painted it red, white and yellow.

3. Now Jamal is building another rocket.

4. It will fly many feet into the air.

5. A parachute will bring the rocket back to Jamal.

6. I am buying a model rocket, too.

B. Complete each sentence with the correct main verb or helping verb in the brackets ( ). Write the word on the line.

1. Kim _____ making a clay vase. (is, has)

2. The clay _____ arrived yesterday. (was, had)

3. I am _____ to watch her work. (go, going)

4. She is _____ a potter's wheel. (used, using)

5. The sculpture _____ go above the fireplace. (will, is)

6. People _____ admired Kim's beautiful vases. (are, have)

C. Write two sentences about something you will do later in the week. Use the future tense helping verb. Be sure to use a main verb and helping verb in each sentence.

1. _____

2. _____

Irregular verbs *do not form the past tense by adding* **-ed**. *They change their form.*

A. **In each sentence, underline the past tense of the verb in the brackets ( ). Then write the past-tense verb on the line.**

1. Jessi told Jackie to be ready early. (tell) _____

2. He was nervous about his science fair project. (is) _____

3. Jackie's friends came to the table. (come) _____

4. They saw the volcano there. (see) _____

5. Jackie knew his speech by heart. (know) _____

6. The sign on the exhibit fell over. (fall) _____

7. The teacher lit the match for Jackie. (light) _____

8. Jackie threw his hands into the air. (throw) _____

B. **Complete each sentence. Write the correct verb on the line.**

> fell   threw   saw   knew

1. Jackie _____ all about volcanoes.

2. He once _____ a real volcano.

3. It _____ ashes and fire into the air.

4. The ashes _____ all over the ground.

C. **Complete each sentence. Use the past-tense form of know in one and the past-tense form of tell in the other.**

1. When I was five, I _____

2. My brother _____

Date: _____

Color the word that is missing from each sentence and write it on the line.

1. We _____ a spelling test yesterday.　taked　took

2. There _____ frost on the ground.　was　were

3. Tommy _____ the Statue of Liberty.　seen　saw

4. How _____ elephants are at the zoo?　much　many

5. Carla _____ her lizard to school.　brought　brang

6. Have you _____ my dog?　seen　saw

7. Alyssa _____ a new pair of skates.　gots　has

8. You _____ supposed to finish your work.　are　is

9. We _____ standing near a snake!　were　was

10. They _____ a worm in the mud.　seen　saw

11. We _____ our winter boots.　wore　weared

12. Is she _____ to come over?　gonna　going

13. _____ your cat climb trees?　Do　Does

14. Rosie _____ cookies to the bake sale.　brang　brought

Adjectives *are words that describe people, places or things. They can help you imagine how something looks, feels, smells, sounds or tastes.*

Make a list of words that describe the object in each bag below.

 Use a paper sack to make a real mystery bag. Place an object in the bag and give describing clues to someone. Can he or she guess the mystery object?

Date: _____

 *An **adjective** is a word that describes a person, place or thing.*

A. Read each sentence. Write the adjective on the line that describes the underlined noun.

1. We live near a sparkling <u>brook.</u> _____

2. It has clear <u>water.</u> _____

3. Large <u>fish</u> swim in the brook. _____

4. Busy <u>squirrels</u> play near the brook. _____

5. You can enjoy breathing in the fresh <u>air</u> near the brook. _____

B. Complete each sentence by adding an adjective.

1. I love _____ apples.

2. I see a _____ ball.

3. I smell _____ flowers.

4. I hear _____ music.

5. I like the _____ taste of pickles.

*The words **a**, **an** and **the** are special adjectives called **articles**. **A** is used before words that begin with a consonant. **An** is used before words that begin with a vowel. **The** is used before either.*

A. Circle the articles in each sentence.

1. The elk, moose and bears grazed in the forest.

2. There was an abundant supply of grass and plants.

3. A bolt of lightning struck a tree and started a fire.

4. Fires have always been an important part of forest ecology.

5. The heat of the summer left the forest very dry.

6. The fires spread over a large area.

7. The helicopters and an airplane spread chemicals on the fire.

8. Firefighters made an attempt to stop the flames.

B. Circle the article in the brackets ( ) that completes each sentence correctly. Then write it on the line.

1. Last summer I visited _____ National Park. (a, an)

2. We took a bus through _____ forests. (an, the)

3. The bus carried us up _____ narrow roads. (a, the)

4. I saw _____ elk grazing on some grass. (a, an)

5. We stayed in _____ old log cabin. (a, an)

6. Deer came up to _____ cabin window. (an, the)

7. We made _____ new friend. (a, an)

8. I wrote my friend _____ letter. (a, an)

Date: _____

 *A **preposition** often helps tell where something is.*

Study the picture. Find each item in the column on the left. Then draw a line to the words that tell where it is. The prepositions are underlined.

What		**Where**
1. chair		(a) <u>above</u> the door
2. bear		(b) <u>on</u> the desk
3. shoe		(c) <u>under</u> the bed
4. plane		(d) <u>behind</u> the trash basket
5. cat		(e) <u>on</u> the bed
6. computer		(f) <u>at</u> the window
7. dog		(g) <u>near</u> the desk
8. poster		(h) <u>over</u> the bed

*A **contraction** is a word that combines two smaller words. An apostrophe is added where letters have been left out. For example, **it is** becomes **it's**.*

A. Read and write each word. Then separate each contraction to write two smaller words.

List Words

1. where's   _____   _____   _____
2. wouldn't   _____   _____   _____
3. you'll   _____   _____   _____
4. haven't   _____   _____   _____
5. we've   _____   _____   _____
6. she's   _____   _____   _____
7. they'll   _____   _____   _____
8. shouldn't   _____   _____   _____
9. that's   _____   _____   _____
10. you've   _____   _____   _____
11. doesn't   _____   _____   _____
12. aren't   _____   _____   _____

B. Circle a set of words that could be replaced with a contraction. Write the list word on the line.

1. We knew we would not be at the game. _____

2. Sydney said that she is going on vacation. _____

3. It does not look like a good day for the beach. _____

4. They will celebrate the team's victory. _____

5. Mom said that you have got to come inside. _____

6. I have not seen the new movie yet. _____

A. Underline the contraction in each sentence. Circle the apostrophe. Then write the contraction on the line.

1. It's time for another adventure. _____

2. We're studying animal habitats. _____

3. They've made a habitat for Bella. _____

4. I'm sure that Bella is gone. _____

5. Wanda thinks that she'll be back. _____

6. They're in favor of going to find Bella. _____

B. Circle the contraction. Then write the two words that make up the contraction.

1. I've gone on this bus before. _____

2. What's the bus doing? _____

3. It's shrinking to the size of a bullfrog. _____

4. The students say they're having fun. _____

5. "I'm hanging on for dear life," Liz said. _____

C. Put the two words together to form a contraction.

1. he + will = _____

2. I + am = _____

3. they + are = _____

4. we + will = _____

5. who + is = _____

6. there + is = _____

Quotation marks *show the exact words of a speaker.* **Commas** *appear between the day and year in a date, between the city and state in a location, and between the lines of an address.*

A. Add quotation marks to show the speaker's exact words.

1. I have a strange case, said Mr Brown.

2. What's strange about it? asked Encyclopedia.

3. Seventeen years ago Mr Hunt found an elephant, began Mr Brown.

4. Where did he find it? asked Mrs Brown.

5. The elephant just appeared in his window, answered Mr Brown.

6. He must have fainted! exclaimed Encyclopedia.

7. No, Mr Hunt bought him, said Mr Brown.

B. Add commas wherever they are needed.

1. I go to the library in Sydney Australia.

2. It is located at 744 George Street Sydney Australia.

3. The last time I was there it was October 8 2012.

4. The books I checked out were due November 22 2012.

5. My cousin Jeb goes to a library at 75 Peachtree Lane Farley Alabama USA.

6. Is it true that J K Rowling once spoke at Harvard University in Boston USA?

7. She spoke there on June 5 2008.

8. She might soon read at 218 Eversholt Street London United Kingdom.

Date: _____

 *A **describing word** makes a sentence more interesting.*

Read the describing words found in the beach balls. Add the describing words to make each sentence more interesting. Write each new sentence.

1. The snow cone sat in the sun.

   melting   bright

   _____

2. Many children ran toward the ocean waves.

   excited   crashing

   _____

3. My friends built a sandcastle.

   new   large

   _____

4. My brother grabbed his beach toys.

   younger   favorite

   _____

5. Our dog tried to catch beach balls.

   playful   flying

   _____

Date: _____

 A sentence is more interesting when it gives exact information.

Replace each **word to make the sentence more exact.**

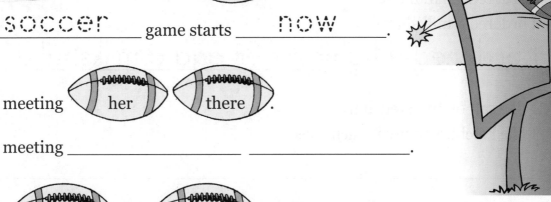

1. The ball game starts soon .

   The _____soccer_____ game starts _____now_____.

2. We are meeting her there .

   We are meeting _____ _____.

3. Let's eat this and that before the game.

   Let's eat _____ and _____ before the game.

4. I hope they score some points.

   I hope _____ score _____ points.

5. They were also there .

   _____ were also _____.

6. He played a good game!

   _____ played a _____ game!

Date: _____

 Sometimes two sentences can be combined to make one sentence.

Sentences that share the same subject seem to go together like ketchup and mustard. Rewrite the sentences by combining their endings with the word *and*.

1. I ordered a hamburger.
   I ordered a milkshake.

   I ordered a hamburger and a milkshake.

2. I like salt on my French fries.
   I like ketchup on my French fries.

   _____

3. My mom makes great cupcakes.
   My mom makes great applesauce.

   _____

4. My dad eats two huge helpings of meat loaf!
   My dad eats two huge helpings of potatoes!

   _____

5. My brother helps set the table.
   My brother helps clean the dishes.

   _____

6. We have cookies for dessert.
   We have ice cream for dessert.

   _____

building a paragraph — writing a topic sentence

Date: _____

> *A topic sentence is sometimes called the* **main idea.**

Read the groups of sentences. Then write a topic sentence that tells the main idea of the paragraph.

1. _____

_____

One reason is that hamsters do not need a lot of attention. Second, hamsters are easy to tame. Last, they are easy to care for.

2. _____

_____

First, spread peanut butter on two pieces of bread. Next, cut a banana into slices and lay them on top of the peanut butter. Then close the two pieces of bread into a sandwich. Last, eat it up!

3. _____

_____

Frogs usually have longer legs and wetter skin than toads do. Many frogs live near a water source of some kind while toads prefer a damp, muddy environment. Frog eggs and toad eggs are different in shape.

Grammar and Vocabulary • L2   59

The sentence that tells the topic of a paragraph is called the **topic sentence**.

Draw a line through the sentence that does not belong with the topic.

1. **Topic: Dogs make great family pets.**

   Dogs have great hearing, which helps them protect a family from danger.

   Most dogs welcome their owners with wagging tails.

   My favorite kind of dog is a boxer.

   Many dogs are willing to play with children in a safe manner.

2. **Topic: The story of the invention of the printing press is interesting.**

   The first printing press was made by Johannes Gutenberg.

   Earlier, books were painted and copied by hand.

   Gutenberg was a goldsmith by profession.

   Old books can be found in libraries.

3. **Topic: Hurricanes are called by different names depending on where they occur.**

   Hurricanes have strong, powerful winds.

   In the Philippines, hurricanes are called baguios.

   Hurricanes are called typhoons in the Far East.

   Australian people use the name willy-willies to describe hurricanes.

A good paragraph has at least three supporting sentences.

Finish the paragraphs below by writing three sentences that support the sentence. Use the points in the box to help you.

> carry people from one country to another
>
> transport important cargo
>
> save people when other types of transport are not available

Airplanes are useful in many ways. First, _____

_____

Second, _____

_____

Third, _____

_____

Date: _____

Sentences can be written in order of beginning (B), middle (M) and ending (E) to make a paragraph.

Write a middle and ending sentence to complete each paragraph.

B   The circus started with a roll of drums and flashing lights.

M   Next, _____

E   Last, _____

B   The tightrope walker stepped into the spotlight.

M   Next, _____

E   Last, _____

B   The lion tamer came on stage.

M   Next, _____

E   Last, _____

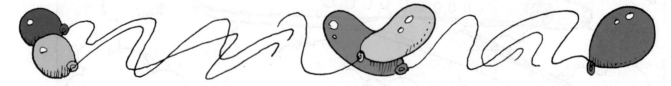

B   The dancing ponies appeared in the center ring.

M   Next, _____

E   Last, _____

*The **closing sentence** retells the topic sentence or main idea of a paragraph.*

Write a closing sentence for each paragraph.

All cyclists should wear helmets while riding their bikes. Many injuries occur to the head in biking accidents. Helmets could help prevent such injuries. Helmets also make cyclists more easily noticed by car drivers.

_____

_____

_____

There are many things to do on a rainy day. If you like to write, you could send a letter to a friend or make a book. If you prefer craft projects, you could make a bookmark or a collage. If you really enjoy games, you could play cards or build a puzzle.

_____

_____

The wheel must be one of the world's most important inventions. First, we would have no means of transportation if it were not for wheels. Second, we would not be able to enjoy many of our favorite pastimes, like in-line skating and riding a bike. Last, it would be very difficult to move heavy objects around without wheels.

_____

_____

_____

*The five parts of a **personal letter** include the date, greeting, body, closing and signature. Notice the punctuation marks that are used in each part.*

August 13, 2003 ⟵ date

greeting ⟶ Dear Gramps,

body ⟶ We had a great fishing trip! Dad caught two bass. I hooked an enormous catfish, but he got away.
I guess Swan Lake is lucky for us. I'll always remember this trip.

Love, ⟵ closing

John ⟵ signature

Write a letter to an out-of-town family member.

_____
(today's date)

_____,

_____

_____

_____

_____

_____

_____,

(your name)

Fill in the bubble next to the correct answer.

1. Which is a complete sentence?

    ○ **A**   Friendly parents

    ○ **B**   My parents are

    ○ **C**   Very famous

    ○ **D**   My parents are friendly and generous.

2. Which type of sentence is the following?
    Look at that horse.

    ○ **A**   telling

    ○ **B**   question

    ○ **C**   exclamation

    ○ **D**   command

3. Which noun is a proper noun?

    ○ **A**   Yellowstone National Park

    ○ **B**   zoo

    ○ **C**   planetarium

    ○ **D**   museum

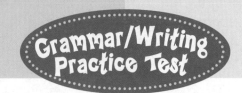

Grammar/Writing Practice Test

Fill in the bubble next to the correct answer.

4. Which sentence is correct?

○ **A**   our teacher is dr Ruffin

○ **B**   Our teacher, Dr ruffin, is from England.

○ **C**   Our teacher, Dr ruffin, is from England.

○ **D**   Our teacher, Dr Ruffin, is from England.

5. Which word is the action verb in the following sentence?
   The villagers happily cheered loudly.

○ **A**   the

○ **B**   happily

○ **C**   cheered

○ **D**   loudly

6. Which pronoun would take the place of "my friends" in the following sentence?
   My friends read a story aloud to the children in the hospital.

○ **A**   it

○ **B**   us

○ **C**   she

○ **D**   they

Fill in the bubble next to the correct answer.

7. Which word is the linking verb in the following sentence?

They are hard workers and wonderful friends.

○ **A**   they

○ **B**   are

○ **C**   and

○ **D**   workers

8. Which word is the simple predicate in the following sentence?

All the children looked at the purple cow with amazement.

○ **A**   looked

○ **B**   all

○ **C**   amazement

○ **D**   children

9. Which word is the simple subject in the following sentence?

Many people visited the museum that day.

○ **A**   many

○ **B**   people

○ **C**   visited

○ **D**   museum

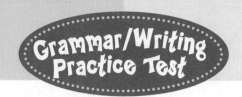

Fill in the bubble next to the correct answer.

10. Read the sentence. Identify the error.

The kids at Elm school had been waiting for a snowstorm?

○ **A**   kids

○ **B**   had been

○ **C**   question mark

○ **D**   correct as is

11. Read the sentence. Identify the error.

they knew school would be canceled if the storm brought a lot of snow.

○ **A**   they

○ **B**   school

○ **C**   canceled

○ **D**   period

12. Read the sentence. Identify the error.

It snowed twelve inches, so school is canceled.

○ **A**   snowed

○ **B**   is

○ **C**   twelve

○ **D**   period

carrot	apple
broom	flower
eggs	crack
drink	drive
sad	happy
dirty	clean
rough	smooth
narrow	wide

nothing	everything
begin	start
fearful	afraid
woods	forest
jam	train
yard	rest
hair	hare
here	weight

wait	sunflower
bathtub	toothpaste
library	circle
square	hexagon
sum	equal
solve	continent
island	ocean
river	regroup

Answer Key

Vocabulary

Page 6
1. carrot, orange, food
2. broom, sweep, clean
3. flowers, leaves, smile
4. ducks, two, quack

Page 7
1. eggs, cracks, three
2. fish, bowl, jump
3. candle, flame, melt
4. boy, drive, wave

Page 8
1. zebra, stripes, animal
2. frog, tongue, fly
3. ghost, white, boo
4. turtle, shell, star

Page 9
1. pull
2. Everything
3. empty
4. inside
5. last
6. play
7. cry
8. noisy

Page 10
1. small
2. outside
3. apart
4. leave
5. stand
6. worse
7. light
8. All

Page 11
1. only
2. keep
3. forest
4. tired
5. happy
6. smelled
7. ripped
8. talked

Page 12
1. small
   tiny
   ~~joyful~~
   little
2. scared
   frightened
   ~~fat~~
   terrified
3. thin
   skinny
   ~~smart~~
   slim
4. chubby
   plump
   ~~terrified~~
   fat
5. nice
   ~~little~~
   lovely
   pleasant
6. ~~empty~~
   huge
   big
   large
7. brave
   daring
   ~~pleasant~~
   bold
8. ~~slim~~
   sad
   unhappy
   upset
9. bare
   ~~large~~
   vacant
   empty
10. ~~hushed~~
    intelligent
    clever
    smart
11. quiet
    ~~upset~~
    soft
    hushed
12. happy
    glad
    ~~bold~~
    joyful

Page 13
1. bark
2. leaf
3. stem
4. root
5. trunk
6. trunk, j
7. bark, a
8. root, g
9. stem, e
10. leaf, d

Page 14
1. bored, board
2. bear, bare
3. chili, chilly
4. pain, pane
5. guessed, guest
6. patience, patients
7. maize, maze
8. hare, hair

Page 15

```
s o l a r s y s t e m p
m m e t e o r j c k l l
o o m o r t i l k o g m a
o s q w e r t k m y b n n
n v s t a r s j e s n b e
  r o c k e t g h t u b t
a s t r o n a u t n v s
g a l a x y f d s a c x
```

Page 16

```
F I R E F I G H T E R D D
A S D R E P W C Q T F O
B A K E R I M A L E A C
X C V B N L P T K C R T
C H E F O O I J H M O
E R T Y U T Z A H E E R
D E N T I S T I G E R D
L A W Y E R J N F R A S
```

Page 17

```
d i f f e r e n c e s q
p w e r e g r o u p u b
l r t y u i o p l k b o
u z a d d f s g h j t r
s x c v n a s u m l r r
w b g e q u a l s u a o
a q m i n u s o h j c w
m a t h i f n d s v t m
```

Page 18
1. add, sum
2. subtract, difference
3. altogether, total
4. have left, how many more
5. equal
6. solve

Page 19

1. Australia
2. Asia
3. Greenland
4. Africa
5. South America
6. Antarctica

Page 20

1. anthers
2. stigma
3. petals
4. style
5. ovary
6. petals
7. stigma
8. anthers
9. ovary
10. style

Page 21

1. head
2. thorax
3. legs
4. stinger
5. antennae
6. eyes
7. wings
8. abdomen
9. head
10. eyes
11. antennae
12. legs,
13. thorax
14. wings
15. abdomen
16. stinger

Page 22

1. responsibility
2. honesty
3. cooperation
4. consideration
5. patience; character

Page 23

1. musician
2. melody
3. composer
4. opera
5. orchestra
6. woodwind
7. conductor
8. rhythm; symphony

Page 24

1. accept
2. dessert
3. angles
4. finale
5. breath
6. loose
7. calendar
8. pasture
9. comma
10. picture

Page 25

1. lab
2. stereo
3. champ
4. movie
5. ref
6. fridge
7. bike
8. ad
9. vet
10. sub
11. gas
12. auto
13. exam
14. photo
15. plane
16. fax
17. phone
18. teen
19. math
20. taxi

Page 26

1. water
2. notes
3. drove
4. river
5. tame
6. month
7. awake
8. women
9. open, shut; hard, soft

Page 27

1. climb
2. least
3. sour
4. see
5. brush
6. sad
7. full

Page 28

1. hat
2. grin
3. tune
4. pan
5. damp
6. glad
7. quick
8. nap

Page 29

1. strong
2. answer
3. play
4. smooth
5. far
6. unsafe
7. late
8. back

Pages 30–31

1. B
2. A
3. C
4. B
5. C
6. B

Grammar/Writing

Page 33

A. 2. Many large paintings; hung on the walls; paintings
3. Maria; saw a painting of an elephant; Maria
4. All the children; looked at the painting; children
5. Paul; pointed to a cat on a leash; Paul
6. His friend; liked the dancing zebra; friend
7. The girls; laughed at the purple cow; girls
8. Many people visited the museum that day; people
9. The bus; took us back to school; bus

B. Review sentences.

Page 34

1. S
2. F
3. S
4. S
5. F
6. F
7. S
8. F
9. F
10. F
11. S
12. S

Page 35

A. 1. Mike and Jody; CS
2. call and email; CP
3. jogs and swims; CP
4. Phil and Jan; CS
5. Juan and Yoshi; CS
6. speak and read; CP
7. Lori, Sam and Beth; CS
8. practiced and presented; CP
9. clapped and smiled; CP
10. The parents and the principal; CS

B. 1. barked and jumped
2. My dad and sister

Page 36
1. S; The sun is the closest star to Earth.
2. S; The sun is not the brightest star.
3. Q; What is the temperature of the sun?
4. S; The sun is a ball of hot gas.
5. Q; How large is the sun?
6. Q; Will the sun ever burn out?

Page 37
A. 1. S   2. S   3. P
   4. S   5. P;
B. 1. baby; sisters   2. nightgown; pockets
   3. hand; fingers   4. baby; parents   5. family; girls
C. fences, train, gates, cow

Page 38
A. 1. doctor, Pat   2. park, France
   3. football, Tangram
B. Review that actions have been
   followed.

Page 39
A. 1. Anna's; S   2. birds'; P
   3. Brad's; S   4. butterfly's; S
   5. turtle's; S   6. chipmunks'; P
   7. animals'; P
B. 1. Carol's   2. Jim's   3. sister's
   4. brother's   5. dad's   6. sneaker's
   7. dog's

Page 40
A. 1. He; S   2. I; S   3. They; P
   4. We; P   5. lt; S
B. 1. It; story; singular   2. she; author; singular
   3. We; My friends and I; plural
   4. They; Two boys; P
C. 1. it   2. it   3. they   4. she

Page 41
A. 1. us   2. it   3. him   4. you
   5. me   6. her   7. them
B. 1. them   2. her   3. it   4. him
   5. us   6. you   7. us

Page 42
A. 2. you; your   3. he; his
   4. she; her   5. it; its
   6. we; our   7. they; their
B. 1. their   2. Her   3. his   4. His
   5. My   6. your   7. Its   8. Our

Page 43
A. 1. cheered   2. added   3. give
   4. serves   5. emptied

B. 1. paraded   2. whispered   3. gobbled
   4. skipped   5. bounced
C. 1. laughed   2. sighed   3. whispered

Page 44
A. 1. fills   2. watches   3. takes
   4. leave   5. go
B. 1. looked   2. stared
   3. walked   4. helped
C. Review sentences.

Page 45
A. 1. was   2. is   3. are
   4. am   5. were
B. 1. past   2. present   3. present
   4. past   5. present
C. 1. am   2. are   3. is

Page 46
A. 1. had; built   2. has; painted
   3. is; building   4. will; fly
   5. will; bring   6. am; buying
B. 1. is   2. had   3. going
   4. using   5. will   6. have
C. Review sentences.

Page 47
A. 1. told   2. was   3. came   4. saw
   5. knew   6. fell   7. lit   8. threw
B. 1. knew   2. saw   3. threw   4. fell
C. Review that sentences include
   "knew" and "told".

Page 48
1. took   2. was   3. saw
4. many   5. brought   6. seen
7. has   8. are   9. were
10. saw   11. wore   12. going
13. Does   14. brought

Page 49
Review lists of adjectives.

Page 50
A. 1. sparkling   2. clear   3. large
   4. busy   5. fresh
B. Review sentences for adjectives.

Page 51
A. 1. the, the   2. an   3. a, a, a
   4. an   5. the, the, the 6. the, a
   7. the, an, the   8. an, the
B. 1. a   2. the   3. the   4. an
   5. an   6. the   7. a   8. a

Page 52

1. g   2. e   3. d   4. h
5. f   6. b   7. c   8. a
Review sentences.

Page 53

A. 1. where is   2. would not
   3. you will   4. have not
   5. we have   6. she is
   7. they will   8. should not
   9. that is   10. you have
   11. does not   12. are not
B. 1. wouldn't   2. she's   3. doesn't
   4. They'll   5. you've   6. haven't

Page 54

A. 1. It's   2. We're   3. They've
   4. I'm   5. she'll   6. They're
B. 1. I've; I have   2. What's; What is
   3. It's; It is   4. they're; they are
   5. I'm; I am
C. 1. he'll   2. I'm   3. they're
   4. we'll   5. who's   6. there's

Page 55

A. 1. "I have a strange case,"
   2. "What's strange about it?"
   3. "Seventeen years ago Mr Hunt found an elephant."
   4. "Where did he find it?"
   5. "The elephant just appeared in the window."
   6. "He must have fainted!"
   7. "No, Mr Hunt bought him,"
B. 1. Sydney, Australia
   2. 744 George Street, Sydney, Australia
   3. October 8, 2012
   4. November 22, 2012
   5. 75 Peachtree Lane, Farley, Alabama, USA
   6. Boston, USA
   7. June 8, 2008
   8. 218 Eversholt Street, London, United Kingdom

Page 56

Sentences may vary.
1. The melting snow cone sat in the bright sun.
2. Many excited children ran toward the crashing ocean waves

3. My new friends built a large sandcastle
4. My younger brother grabbed his favorite beach toys.
5. Our playful dog tried to catch flying beach balls.

Page 57

Review suitable words.

Page 58

2. I like salt and ketchup on my French fries.
3. My mom makes great cup cakes and applesauce.
4. My dad eats two huge helpings of meat loaf and potatoes!
5. My brother helps set the table and clean the dishes.
6. We have cookies and ice cream for dessert.

Page 59

1. Why hamsters make good pets
2. How to make a peanut-butter and banana sandwich
3. The difference between frogs and toads

Page 60

1. My favorite kind of dog is a boxer.
2. Old books can be found in libraries.
3. Hurricanes have strong, powerful winds.

Page 61

Review paragraphs for 3 supporting sentences.

Page 62

Review that paragraphs include a clear beginning, middle and ending.

Page 63

Review closing sentences.

Page 64

Review letter for necessary parts.

Pages 65–73

1. D   2. D   3. A   4. D
5. C   6. D   7. B   8. A
9. B   10. C   11. A   12. B

SCHOLASTIC

Learning Express

Congratulations!

I, _____

am a Scholastic Superstar!

Paste a photo or draw a picture of yourself.

I have completed Grammar and Vocabulary L2.

Presented on _____